First World War
and Army of Occupation
War Diary
France, Belgium and Germany

57 DIVISION
171 Infantry Brigade
King's (Liverpool Regiment)
2/5 Battalion
1 September 1915 - 29 February 1916

WO95/2983/1

The Naval & Military Press Ltd
www.nmarchive.com
Published in association with The National Archives

Published by

The Naval & Military Press Ltd

Unit 10 Ridgewood Industrial Park,

Uckfield, East Sussex,

TN22 5QE England

Tel: +44 (0) 1825 749494

www.naval-military-press.com

www.nmarchive.com

This diary has been reprinted in facsimile from the original. Any imperfections are inevitably reproduced and the quality may fall short of modern type and cartographic standards.

© **Crown Copyright**
Images reproduced by permission of The National Archives, London, England, 2015.

Contents

Document type	Place/Title	Date From	Date To
Heading	WO95/2983/1 57 Div 171 Infantry Bde 2/5 Btw Kings Liverpool Regt Aug 1915-Feb 1916		
Heading	57th Division 171st Infy Bde 2-5th Bn King's L'pools 1915 Aug-1916 Feb And 1917 Feb-1918 Jan		
Miscellaneous	Intelligence Summary Of 2/5th Battalion "The King's" (Liverpool Regiment)	03/09/1915	03/09/1915
Miscellaneous	2/5th Battalion "The King's" (L'pool Regt.)		
Heading	War Diary 2/5th L'Pool Rgt 1st/30th Sept 1915		
War Diary	Canterbury	01/09/1915	30/09/1915
Heading	War Diary October 1915 2/5th K.L.R. From 1st October 1915 To 31st October 1915		
War Diary	Canterbury	01/10/1915	31/10/1915
Heading	War Diary Of 2/5th Battalion "The King's" (Liverpool Regiment) From 1st To 30th November 1915		
War Diary	Canterbury	01/11/1915	01/12/1915
Heading	War Diary Of 2/5th Battalion "The King's" (Liverpool Regiment) From 1st To 31st December 1915		
War Diary	Canterbury	01/12/1915	31/12/1915
Heading	War Diary Of 2/5th Battalion "The King's" (Liverpool Regiment) From 1st To 31st January 1916		
War Diary	Canterbury	01/01/1916	31/01/1916
Heading	War Diary Of 2/5th Battalion "The King's" (Liverpool Regiment) From 1st To 29th February 1916		
War Diary	Canterbury	01/02/1916	29/02/1916

WO95/2983/1

57 DIV, 171 INFANTRY BDE

2/5 BTN KINGS LIVERPOOL REGT

Aug 1915 - Feb 1916

57TH DIVISION
171ST INFY BDE

2-5TH BN KING'S L'POOLS

~~FEB 1917 - MAR 1918~~

1915 AUG - 1916 FEB
AND
1917 FEB - 1918 JAN

DISBANDED

CONFIDENTIAL.

INTELLIGENCE SUMMARY

of

2/5th Battalion "The King's" (Liverpool Regiment.)

from

1st to 31st August 1915.

CANTERBURY,

3rd September 1915.

UNIT :- 2/5th Battalion "The King's" (L'pool Regt.)

BRIGADE :- 171st Infantry Brigade, T.F.

DIVISION :- 57th (West Lancs.) Division.

MOBILIZATION CENTRE :- Liverpool.

TEMPORARY WAR STATION :- Canterbury.

STATIONS SINCE OCCUPIED SUBSEQUENT TO CONCENTRATION :- Blackpool and Canterbury.

(a) MOBILIZATION :- On Formation.

(b) CONCENTRATION AT WAR STATION :- (Including Railway Moves.) None since move from Blackpool to Canterbury, on 1st March 1915.

(c) ORGANIZATION FOR DEFENCE :- (Including vulnerable points.) The Battalion is part of the 171st Infantry Brigade.

(d) TRAINING :- Battalion Training and Company Training. Brigade Field Operations. Attention has been given to Bayonet Fighting and to a limited extent the throwing of hand grenade

(e) DISCIPLINE :- Very Good.

(f) ADMINISTRATION :-

    1. Medical Services. — Medical Officer is temporarily attached.

    2. Veterinary Services. — Rendered through 57th Division.

    3. Supply Services. — A.S.C. of 57th Division.

    4. Transport Services. — Partly the Unit's own 1st Line Transport and partly A.S.C.

    5. Ordnance Services. — D.A.D.O.S. Canterbury.

    6. Billeting. — Canterbury.

    7. Channels of correspondence in routine matters. — 171st Infantry Brigade.

    8. Range Construction. — None under construction, but Musketry carried out at Sandwich and Deal.

    9. Supply of Remounts. — Officers' Chargers were supplied through 3/1st Liverpool Infantry Brigade and certain Horses were taken over from the Imperial Service Unit.

(g) REORGANIZATION OF T.F. INTO IMPERIAL SERVICE.

> On the formation of the
> 43rd Provisional Battalion
> 6 Officers and 333 N.C.O's and
> men (Home Service) were transferred
> from this Unit.
> 123 N.C.O.'s and men have since been
> returned under the heading
> Foreign Service - Medically Unfit.

(h) PREPARING OF UNITS FOR IMPERIAL SERVICE.

> Regarding any drafts required
> special attention is being given to
> Physical Training, Musketry and
> Bayonet Fighting, including
> Final Assault Practice.

[signature]

                                  Lieut.-Colonel.
O.C. 2/5th Battalion "The King's" (L'pool Regt)

Confidential 171 BDE

War Diary
2/5th L'pool Regt.

1st/30th Sept. 1915

Army Form C. 2118

WAR DIARY
or
INTELLIGENCE SUMMARY

(Erase heading not required.)

Instructions regarding War Diaries and Intelligence Summaries are contained in F.S. Regs., Part II. and the Staff Manual respectively. Title Pages will be prepared in manuscript.

Place	Date	Hour	Summary of Events and Information	Remarks and references to Appendices
CANTERBURY	1915. September.			
	1	9 a.m.	Battalion Training.) 1 N.C.O. and 20 men proceeded to Old Park, Canterbury, for Course of	
		2 p.m.	Company Training.) Instruction in Horsemanship.	
	2	8 a.m.	Brigade Field Operations. 2 Riflemen transferred to 43rd Provisional Battalion, Sheringham.	
			1 Rfn. reported for duty from Administrative Centre, 5th K.L.R.	
	3	9 a.m.	Route March with Transport.	
		8 p.m.	Night Operations.	
	4	—	Usual Routine. 1 Rifleman transferred from 43rd Provisional Battalion, Sheringham.	
	5	9 a.m.	Church Parade.	
	6	—	Usual Routine. 1 Rfn. transferred from 43rd Prev. Bn.	
			1 N.C.O. proceeded to Aylesford for Course of Instruction in Veterinary and Farriery.	
	7	9 a.m.	Route March with Transport.) 1 Officer and 1 N.C.O. proceeded to Godstone for Course of Instruction	
			Night Operations.) Grenadier's.	
	8	—	Usual Routine. 9 men of 2/6th Bn. K.L.R. attached to 2/5th K.L.R. for Machine Gun Course	
			rejoined their Unit on the 8th September.	
			Sergeant Jones discharged, War Office Authority to be Commissioned.	
			Court Martial held for trial of Rfn. O'Neill, No. 3373, 2/5th K.L.R.	
	9	9 a.m.	Battalion Field Operations. 1 N.C.O. and 10 men returned from Transport Course at Old Park. C'bury.	
	10	10 a.m.	FIRE ALARM AT HOTHE COURT FARM. Battalion were in attendance all day.	
	11	9 a.m.	Battalion Training. C.S.M. Inst. Goodall, Army Gymnastic Staff, proceeded to Bedford as	
			Instructor to 2/1st Welsh Division, finished duty with 2/5th K.L.R.	
			as from the 10th September.	
	12	9 a.m.	Church Parade. 1 Officer returned from Course of Instruction in Telephony at Ramsgate.	
	13	—	Usual Routine. 2 Officers proceeded to Cambridge for General Course of Instruction (Elementary).	
	14	9 a.m.	Route March with Transport. 1 Officer reported for Duty (Appointment.)	
			1 N.C.O and 20 men returned from Course of Horsemanship, Old Park.	
	15	9 a.m.	Alarm Parade and Inspection. "A" Company 2/5th K.L.R. in conjunction with a Company of the	
		2 p.m.	Company Training. 2/8th (Irish) Bn. K.L.R. proceeded to Chartham Downs on Outpost	
			Duty in Connection with the Brigade Field Operations of the 16th Sept.,	
			the Company left Canterbury at about 7-30 p.m.	
	16	7-30 a.m.	Brigade Field Operations, Chartham Downs. 1 Officer returned for Duty from Advanced Course	
			of Instruction at South Harrow.	
	17	9 a.m.	Battalion Training. 1 Officer Joined for Duty (Attached.)	
		8 p.m.	Night Operations.	

J.B.C. & A.   A.D.S.S./Forms/C. 2118.

Army Form C. 2118

WAR DIARY
or
INTELLIGENCE SUMMARY
(Erase heading not required.)

Instructions regarding War Diaries and Intelligence Summaries are contained in F. S. Regs., Part II. and the Staff Manual respectively. Title Pages will be prepared in manuscript.

Place	Date	Hour	Summary of Events and Information	Remarks and references to Appendices
CANTERBURY	1915 September.			
	18	9 a.m.	Company Training. 18 N.C.Os. and men of the Headquarters Staff, 171st Inf. Brigade attached to 2/5th K.L.R. for Rations as from the 18th September. 1 Rifleman of the Headquarters Staff attached to 2/5th K.L.R. for Pay, Billet, and Rations as from the 18th September 1915.	
	19	9 a.m.	Church Parade. Transport Officer returned from General Course of Instruction at Chelsea. Transport Officer proceeded to Woolwich for Course of Instruction in Transport Duties.	
	20	-	Usual Routine. 5 Officers joined for Duty (Attached). 1 Officer and 1 N.C.O. returned from Grenadier 1 N.C.O. returned from Course of Inst. Course at Godstone. Vet. and Farriery at Aylesford.	
	21	9 a.m.	Route March with Transport. 1 Officer and 1 N.C.O. proceeded to Wrotham, Infantry Pioneer Course.	
		2 p.m.	Coy. Training.	
	22	9 a.m.	Coy. Training. 4 N.C.Os. commenced Brigade Course of Instruction for N.C.Os. Sessions House	
		2 p.m.	Brigade Field Operations. 1 Rfn. Proceeded to Aylesbury for Course of Cold Shoeing.	
	23	8 a.m.	Brigade Field Operations (continued from 22nd Sept.	
	24	9 a.m.	Battalion Training and Trench Digging.	
		8 p.m.	Night Work, Final Assault Practice.	
	25	9 a.m.	Trench Digging (Rough Common.)	
		2 p.m.	Company Training.	
	26	9 a.m.	Church Parade.	
	27	9 a.m.	Battalion Training and Trench Digging.	
		2 p.m.	Company Training.	
	28	9 a.m.	Route March with Transport.	
		2 p.m.	Company Training. 1 Rifleman proceeded to Middlewick for Cookery Course.	
	29	9 a.m.	Battalion Training.	
		8 p.m.	Practice Fire Alarm.	
	30	9 a.m.	Trench Digging all Day. (Rough Common.	

Confidential

War Diary
October 1915

2/5th K.L.R.

From 1st October 1915
to
31st October 1915

2/5th Bn. "THE KING'S" (L'POOL REGT.)

Army Form C. 2118

Instructions regarding War Diaries and Intelligence
Summaries are contained in F.S. Regs., Part II.
and the Staff Manual respectively. Title Pages
will be prepared in manuscript.

WAR DIARY
or
INTELLIGENCE SUMMARY
(Erase heading not required.)

Place	Date	Hour	Summary of Events and Information	Remarks and references to Appendices
CANTERBURY.	1915. October.			
	1	9 a.m.	Battalion Training-) Lieut.Col S.S.G.Cohen assumed command vice Lieut.Col G.Rippon.	
		8 p.m.	Night Operations.)	
	2	-	Usual Routine.	
	3	9 a.m.	Church Parade.	
	4	9 a.m.	Trench Digging) 1 N.C.O proceeded to Aldershot for Physical Training and Bayonet Fighting	
		8 p.m.	Night Operations) Course.	
			Inspection of Transport	
			Lieut Williams returned from Transport Officer's Course at Woolwich.	
	5	-	Usual Routine. 5 Rfn transferred to 43rd Provisional Battalion, Weybourne.	
	6	-	Usual Routine	
	7	-	Usual Routine.	
	8	-	Usual Routine. 2 Officers, 1 N.C.O and 25 Rfn proceeded to Sandwich for Machine Gun practice.	
	9	9 a.m.	Route March with Transport.	
	10	9 a.m.	Church Parade.	
	11	-	Usual Routine. Bug.A.L.Roberts discharged King's Regs 392 (vi) (a).	
	12	9 a.m.	Route March with Transport.) 4 attached Officers rejoined their Battalion, viz., 15th (Service)	
		2 p.m.	Company Training) Battalion King's Liverpool Regt.	
	13	9 a.m.	Battalion Training	
		2 p.m.	Inspection of Munition volunteers at Old Park, Canterbury.	
	14	-	Usual Routine. 2nd Lieut Rimmer and 1 L'cpl proceeded to Wrotham for Infantry Pioneer Course.	
			2nd Lieut.Bescoby)	
			2nd Lieut.Kennett) Returned from Course of Instruction at Cambridge University.	
			36 men selected for munitions work.	
	15	9 a.m.	Battalion Training) 1 N.C.O and 6 men commenced Course of Instruction in Horsemastership Old Park	
		3 p.m.	Fire Alarm Parade) 2nd Lieut Hughes returned from Pioneer Course at Wrotham.	
		8 p.m.	Night Operations) 4108 Rfn Frank declared a deserter as from 4.10.15.	
	16	-	Usual Routine Rfn Murray discharged King's Regs para 392 (vi) (a).	
	17	9 a.m.	Church Parade	
	18	9 a.m.	Battalion Training)	
		8 p.m.	Night Operations.) Captain Leslie proceeded to Course of Instruction at Cambridge	
	19	9 a.m.	Battalion Training) 1 N.C.O proceeded to Wrotham for Grenadier Course.	
		2 p.m.	Company Training) 1 Rfn transferred to 43rd Provisional Battalion,Weybourne.	
	20	5.30 p.m.	Lecture by Brigade Major.) No 4099 Rfn Brennan declared a deserter.	
	21	8.30 a.m.	Route March (All day).	
		-	Usual Routine.	

2/5th Bn. "THE KING'S" (L'POOL REGT.)

Army Form C. 2118

WAR DIARY
or
INTELLIGENCE SUMMARY
(Erase heading not required.)

Instructions regarding War Diaries and Intelligence Summaries are contained in F. S. Regs., Part II. and the Staff Manual respectively. Title Pages will be prepared in manuscript.

Place	Date	Hour	Summary of Events and Information	Remarks and references to Appendices
CANTERBURY.	1915 October.			
	22	9 a.m. Battalion Training) 2 p.m. Company Training)	Rfn Anwyl discharged as from 25/9/15. W.O. authority to be commissioned.	
	23	— Usual Routine.		
	24	9 a.m. Church Parade.		
	25	9 a.m. Battalion Training.) 2 p.m. Company Training)	Lieut Heard commenced advanced Course at Camberley. 2nd Lieut Hughes commenced Course of Instruction at Hertford. Rfn Brennan rejoined from desertion. C-S-M Pierce transferred to the 43rd Provisional Battalion, Weybourne.	
	26	9 a.m. Battalion Training in Physical Training and Bayonet Fighting under C-S)-M Smith. 2 p.m. Company Training. Officers and N.C.O's "Refresher" course in Physical Training.		
	27	9 a.m. Route March with Transport.) 4 N.C.O's commenced class at Sessions House, under Sgt Brumhill. 2 p.m. Company Training.) 5.30 p.m. Fire Alarm Parade.		
	28	9 a.m. Battalion Training) 2 p.m. Company Training)	36 men, under 19 transferred to the 43rd Provisional Battalion, Weybourne. Lieut.G.L.Taylor appointed Brigade Machine Gun Officer and struck off the strength of this Unit. Lieut.H.C.Moxon appointed Machine Gun Officer vice Lieut G.L.Taylor. 2nd Lieut H.H.Whitehouse taken on strength on transfer from the Territorial Force Reserve General List.	
	29	9 a.m. Battalion Training.) 5.30 p.m. Night Operations) (Final Assault)		
	30	— Usual Routine.	1 N.C.O returned from Grenadier Course at Wrotham.	
	31	9 a.m. Church Parade. 11.15 a.m. Special parade for Jews.		

S. Manley Cohen
Lieut. Colonel,
Commanding 2/5th Battn. "The King's" (Liverpool Regt.)

C O N F I D E N T I A L.

War Diary
~~INTELLIGENCE SUMMARY~~

of

2/5th Battalion "The King's" (Liverpool Regiment).

from

1st to 30th November 1915.

CANTERBURY,

4th December 1915.

Army Form C. 2118

WAR DIARY
or
INTELLIGENCE SUMMARY

(Erase heading not required.)

Instructions regarding War Diaries and Intelligence Summaries are contained in F. S. Regs., Part II. and the Staff Manual respectively. Title Pages will be prepared in manuscript.

Place	Date	Hour	Summary of Events and Information	Remarks and references to Appendices
	1915 November October			
CANTERBURY	1	9 a.m. 2 p.m.	Battition Training } 2/Lt Bescoby commenced course in Trench Warfare at Maidstone. Company Training } 2 men transferred to 43rd Provisional Battalion. Usual Routine. Rfn Gribbin declared a deserter.	
	2	—	Usual Routine. 2/Lt Pownall commenced Grenadier course at Godstone.	
	3	—	Usual Routine. Rfn Walker discharged. King's Regs 392(vl) a.	
	4	8.30 a.m.	Field Operations, in conjunction with 2/6th K.L.R. at Whitstable. Attack practice. 1 N.C.O and 5 men commenced course in Horsemastership at Old Park. Rfn Daniels transferred to the 43rd Provisional Battalion.	
	5	—	Usual Routine.	
	6	5 p.m.	Lecture by Brigade Major on Horsemastership. Usual Routine Rfn Dawson & Rfn Goddard declared deserters. 4 men transferred to the 43rd Provisional Battalion.	
	7	—	Church Parade.	
	8	—	Usual Routine. 1 Officer and 4 other ranks proceeded on special duty to Barham. Corporal Davies commenced Infantry Pioneer Course at Wrotham.	
	9	—	Usual Routine	
	10	—	Usual Routine.	
	11	8 a.m.	Field Operations at Barham. 3 additional men selected for munition work.	
	12	—	Usual Routine.	
	13	—	Usual Routine. Rfn Lewthwaite discharged King's Regs 392 (vl) a. Rfn Rea and Rfn Willis declared deserters.	
	15	9 a.m.	Battalion Training. Cpl Johnson discharged to be commissioned.	
	16	5.30 p.m 7 a.m. 9 a.m. 5 p.m.	Night Operations (Outpost work). 4 senior N.C.O's commenced course of instruction (Brigade.) Physical Training under supervision of C.S.M. SMITH? Army Gymnastic Staff. Bayonet fighting " " Alarm Parade. Rfn Cooper released to civil employ. 2 men commenced course in cookery at Dartford.	
	17	—	Usual Routine. 1 Officer and 1 N.C.O commenced course in Trench Warfare at Maidstone. Transport inspected by Major-General Landon.	
	18	—	Usual Routine. Rfn Truby transferred to 2/10th King's Liverpool Regt.	
	19	5.30 p.m.	Lecture by Brigade Major on Horsemastership. Rfn Jones discharged to re-enlist into 21st K.L.R.	

1875 Wt. W593/826 1,000,000 4/15 J.B.C. & A. A.D.S.S./Forms/C. 2118.

Army Form C. 2118

WAR DIARY
or
INTELLIGENCE SUMMARY

(Erase heading not required.)

Instructions regarding War Diaries and Intelligence Summaries are contained in F. S. Regs., Part II. and the Staff Manual respectively. Title Pages will be prepared in manuscript.

Place	Date	Hour	Summary of Events and Information	Remarks and references to Appendices
CANTERBURY.	1915. ~~October~~ November			
	20	7 a.m.	Physical Training under supervision of C.S.M.Smith,Army Gymnastic Staff.	
		9 a.m.	Bayonet Fighting " " " " "	
	21	–	525 .303 Rifles received from Weedon, and Japanese Rifles returned.	
	22	–	1 Officer and 1 N.C.O commenced Grenadier Course at Godstone. Usual Routine. 2/Lieut Miller commenced course at Pembroke College, Cambridge. Sgt MacGowan commenced course at Chelsea Barracks.	
	23	10 a.m.	Inspection by G.O.C-in-C. Rfn Townsend commenced course in Cold shoeing at Bermondsey. Rfn Kneale released to civil employ.	
	24	10 a.m.	Inspection by Major-General Dickson, Inspector of Infantry, at Rough Common.	
		8 p.m.	Fire Alarm Parade.	
	25	–	Usual Routine.	
	26	–	Usual Routine.	
		5.30 p.m.	Night work consisting of concentration march to Chartham. 2 Officers and 75 other ranks proceeded to Deal on special duty with Kent Cyclists.	
	27	–	Usual Routine. 3619 Rfn Wilson– death by gunshot wound.	
	29	–	Usual Routine. Captain Ambler commenced course in Trench Warfare at Maidstone. Sgt Flynne commenced Physical Training and Bayonet Fighting course at Aldershot.	
	30	–	Usual Routine.	
Dec.		5 p.m.	Lecture by Brigade Major on "Fire discipline and Fire Control". 1704 Rfn Wilson released to civil employ.	
	1	–	Usual Routine. 2577 Rfn Henshaw commenced course at School of Farriery at Woolwich. 4 senior N.C.O's commenced course at Sessions House (Brigade).	

Lieut. Colonel,
Commanding 2/5th Battn. "The King's (Liverpool Regt.)

CONFIDENTIAL.

War Diary

~~INTELLIGENCE~~ SUMMARY

of

2/5th Battalion "The King's" (Liverpool Regiment).

from

1st to 31st December 1915.

CANTERBURY,

4th January 1916.

WAR DIARY or INTELLIGENCE SUMMARY

Army Form C. 2118

Instructions regarding War Diaries and Intelligence Summaries are contained in F.S. Regs., Part II. and the Staff Manual respectively. Title Pages will be prepared in manuscript.

(Erase heading not required.)

Place	Date	Hour	Summary of Events and Information	Remarks and references to Appendices
Canterbury	December			
	1		Usual routine. 2577 R/p Henshaw Commenced Course at School of Farriery, Woolwich	A/D
	2	8.0 a.m.	Brigade Field Operations (Concentration march on Canterbury).	A/D
	3		Usual routine. Inspection of Transport by O.C. No 3 Company 57th (West Lanc) Divisional Train A.S.C.	A/D
	4		Usual routine. 4 men released to civil employ for munition work.	A/D
	6		Usual routine. R/p Clements Commenced Course in "Repair of Service Rifles" at Woolwich	A/D
	7		Usual routine.	A/D
	8		Usual routine.	A/D
	9	8.0 a.m.	Field Operations under command of Lt. Col. Fletcher, 2/6th King's Liverpool Regt. Abandoned at 1.0 p.m. owing to wet weather. 2 men released to civil employ for munition work.	A/D
	10		Usual routine.	A/D
		9.30 a.m.	Night work at Chatham. Convoy attempted to break through between Chatham & Canterbury	A/D
		6.0 p.m.	via Sittingbourne and Stone Street. Convoy consisted of "D" Company & Transport. Remainder of Battalion holding ground between these roads.	A/D
	11		Usual routine.	A/D
	13	9.30 a.m.	Battalion training.	A/D
		6.0 p.m.	Night Operation at Rough Common. Battalion exercised in Bayonet Fighting & Final Assault Practice. 92 men transferred to 3/5th King's Liverpool Regt. to reduce establishment to minimum number	A/D
	14	9.30 a.m.	Battalion Training. 16 details of 1/57th (West Lanc) Divisional Cyclist Coy attached to this Unit. 600.	A/D
		2.0 p.m.	Company Training. pending release for munition work. 1 man released to civil employ. 2/Lt. Stoltroin & other ranks relieved Civil Govt on special duty at Barham	A/D

1875 Wt: W593/826 1,000,000 4/15 J.B.C. & A. A.D.S.S./Forms/C. 2118.

WAR DIARY
or
INTELLIGENCE SUMMARY

(Erase heading not required.)

Army Form C. 2118

Instructions regarding War Diaries and Intelligence Summaries are contained in F.S. Regs., Part II. and the Staff Manual respectively. Title Pages will be prepared in manuscript.

Place	Date	Hour	Summary of Events and Information	Remarks and references to Appendices
Canterbury	December			
	15	—	Usual routine.	M.S.
	16	9.0 a.m.	Battalion Field Operations. Attack and defence.	M.S.
	17	2.15 p.m.	Alarm Practice. L/Cpl Rhodes discharged, medically unfit.	M.S.
	18	—	Usual routine. I have released to civil employ.	M.S.
	20	7.30 a.m.	Physical Training under Supervision of Company Sgt Major Smith, Army Gymnastic Staff.	M.S.
		9.30 a.m.	Bayonet Fighting & Final Assault Practice at Rough Common under -do-	M.S.
	21	—	Usual routine.	M.S.
	22	—	Usual routine. 4066 Pte James declared a deserter.	M.S.
	23	9.30 a.m.	Battalion Training. ½ Holiday.	M.S.
	24		Holidays.	
	25			M.S.
	26			M.S.
	27	—	Pte Stewart commenced course in "Cold Shoeing" at Bermondsey.	
	28	5.45 p.m.	Fire Alarm Practice.	M.S.
	29	2.0 p.m.	Inspection by Lieut. General Woolcombe.	M.S.
			"A" Company in Company Drill	
			"B" Company in Bayonet fighting	
			"C" Company in Physical Drill	
			"D" Company in musketry.	
	30	—	Battalion Field Operations.	M.S.
	31	—	Usual routine.	M.S.
		6.0 p.m.	Night Operations. Marching by night.	M.S.

J. Carlyle Cohen
Lieut. Colonel,
Commanding 2/5th Battn. "The King's" (Liverpool Regt.)

CONFIDENTIAL.

WAR   DIARY.

of

2/5th Battalion "The King's" (Liverpool Regiment).

from

1st to 31st January 1916.

——— ———

C ANTERBURY.
    4th February 1916.

Army Form C. 2118

WAR DIARY
or
INTELLIGENCE SUMMARY
(Erase heading not required.)

Instructions regarding War Diaries and Intelligence Summaries are contained in F. S. Regs., Part II. and the Staff Manual respectively. Title Pages will be prepared in manuscript.

Place	Date	Hour	Summary of Events and Information	Remarks and references to Appendices
Canterbury	1916 Jan.			
	1.		nil	do
	2.		nil	do
	3.		nil	do
	4.		nil	do
	5.		nil	do
	6.		nil	do
	7.		nil	do
	8.		nil	do
	9.		nil	do
	10.		nil	do
	11.	3.0 p.m.	General Alarm Parade	do
	12.		nil	do
	13.		nil	do
	14.		nil	do
	15.		nil	do
	16.		nil	do
	17.		nil	do
	18.		nil	do
	19.		nil	do
	20.		nil	do

Army Form C. 2118

WAR DIARY
or
INTELLIGENCE SUMMARY

(Erase heading not required.)

Instructions regarding War Diaries and Intelligence Summaries are contained in F. S. Regs., Part II. and the Staff Manual respectively. Title Pages will be prepared in manuscript.

Place	Date	Hour	Summary of Events and Information	Remarks and references to Appendices
Canterbury	1916 Jan. 22		29 Recruits joined under the "Group" System.	SS
	23		Nil.	SS
	24	3pm.	Fire Alarm Parade (Divisional)	SS
	25		13 Recruits joined under the "Group" System.	SS
	26	8pm	Fire Alarm Parade.	SS
			15 Recruits joined.	SS
	27		16 Recruits joined.	SS
	28		Nil.	SS
	29		6 Recruits joined	SS
	30		Nil.	SS
	31		Nil.	SS

MacLaughlan Lieut. Colonel,
Commanding 2/5th Battn. "The King's" (Liverpool Regt.)

CONFIDENTIAL.

WAR   DIARY.

of

2/5th. Battalion, "The King's" (Liverpool Regiment.).

from

1st. to 29th. February, 1916.

————

CANTERBURY,
     4th. March, 1916.

Army Form C. 2118

WAR DIARY
or
INTELLIGENCE SUMMARY
(Erase heading not required.)

Instructions regarding War Diaries and Intelligence Summaries are contained in F. S. Regs., Part II. and the Staff Manual respectively. Title Pages will be prepared in manuscript.

Place	Date	Hour	Summary of Events and Information	Remarks and references to Appendices
Canterbury	1916 Feb.			
	1		nil	nil
	2		nil	nil
	3		3 recruits joined under the "Scout" system	nil
	4		nil	nil
	5		nil	nil
	6		nil	nil
	7		nil	nil
	8		nil	nil
	9		nil	nil
	10		nil	nil
	11		Lieut. E.L. Harrison. Sols Coast Volunteers, transferred, attached for duty.	nil
	12		nil	nil
	13		Sgt. Instructor Parkinson. Army Gymnastic Staff. attached, for training Battalion in Bayonet Fighting &c	nil
	14			
	15	10.15pm	General Alarm Parade.	nil
	16		nil	nil
	17		nil	nil
	18		nil	nil
	19		nil	nil
	20		nil	nil
	21		nil	nil
	22		nil	nil

1875   Wt. W593/826 1,000,000 4/15 J.B.C. & A. A.D.S.S./Forms/C.2118.

Army Form C. 2118

WAR DIARY
or
INTELLIGENCE SUMMARY
(Erase heading not required.)

Instructions regarding War Diaries and Intelligence Summaries are contained in F. S. Regs., Part II. and the Staff Manual respectively. Title Pages will be prepared in manuscript.

Place	Date	Hour	Summary of Events and Information	Remarks and references to Appendices
Canterbury	1916. Feb.			
	23.		hie. 1 recruit joined.	ms
	24.	11:15am	Battalion received order. "Prepare to move" from 171st Infantry Brigade. All arrangements made to be ready at short notice.	ms
	25		hie	ms
	26		hie 1 recruit joined. Armourer Sgt Littlewood taken on strength.	ms
	27		hie	ms
	28		hie	ms
	29		hie	ms

Stanley Wren, Lieut. Colonel,
Commanding 2/5th Battn. "The King's" (Liverpool Regt.)

www.ingramcontent.com/pod-product-compliance
Lightning Source LLC
Chambersburg PA
CBHW081507160426
43193CB00014B/2611